Wolf Biermann: Poems and Ballads

The poems and ballads in this collection first
appeared in German under the following titles:
Die Drahtharfe, Verlag Klaus Wagenbach, Berlin 1965;
Mit Marx- und Engelszungen, Verlag Klaus Wagenbach,
Berlin 1968; *Für meine Genossen*, Verlag Klaus
Wagenbach, Berlin 1973.

This edition first published 1977 by Pluto Press Limited
Unit 10 Spencer Court, 7 Chalcot Road, London NW1 8LH

ISBN 0 904383 60 1 paperback
    0 904383 61 X hardback

Designed by Tom Sullivan
Music transcribed by Tess Wickham

Printed in Great Britain by Latimer Trend & Company Ltd Plymouth

Wolf Biermann

Wolf Biermann: Poems and Ballads

translated from the German
by Steve Gooch

Pluto  Press

Contents

Contents

Wolf Biermann to Stuart Hood,
East Berlin, October 1974

Although everyone is agreed that art is something unnecessary and might almost be defined as the expression of immodest, cheeky, arrogant, self-indulgent gaiety, such as can only flourish when rooted in the assured fulfillment of human needs, yet at the same time we have, almost involuntarily, the comic desire to achieve – by means of this unnecessary art – all that is most necessary, most important and most fundamental for the life of society and for human existence. In this respect art – or rather artists in their own view of themselves waver between two extreme attitudes: that of excessive modesty and that of excessive arrogance with regard to society's need for art. These are two ways of looking at things – ways which are in danger of making each other ridiculous and which nevertheless are very closely linked. That is to say we want – in almost beggarly modesty – to do no more than entertain and, at the same time, with terrifying immodesty, to set the whole world to rights. And between these two ways of seeing things there is a close connection. That art cannot set the world to rights is something that everybody will readily agree and will laugh at the idea that anyone should even think so. But at the same time, art always behaves as if it could do just that and preserves within itself, in a touching way, that dream of mankind, that it might bring about those great changes, which in our time have become more possible than usual and more necessary than usual – the dream that men have the confidence in themselves to be able to bring them about. Art belongs to those realms of the human spirit in which man articulates and preserves these hopes and does not lose them.

We have all more or less conceited, high-pitched hopes and wishes with regard to changes in society, and people naturally keep asking the painful question: 'What influence can songs have on the social process?' Is it not ridiculous? Is it not – as it says in the Bible – vanity and a waste of breath? What can songs do? I believe that, if tomorrow, in the German Democratic Republic, the most popular brand of cigarettes were sold out in the shops, then the shock society suffered would be greater than if ten poets hanged themselves. That sounds a little too overwhelmingly gloomy. What I am trying to say, in drastic terms, is that one cannot move the world with songs. But when the world itself moves, songs can be born, and when songs are born which give political and poetical expression to passions and hopes and feelings, then a song can have an extraordinarily reinforcing effect. It confirms. It brings individuals together. They say: 'Oh, he feels like that too, he thinks like that too.' People encourage each other by singing a song with the political content of which they agree. At the same time they are generous, they are not petty – they often sing songs in which there are things with which they are not in complete agreement, or things they haven't even thought about. As a child I sang all our workers' songs and didn't understand even half the words. Yet the songs were good because they produced a feeling of solidarity in me – that I was not alone. They produce, to put it this way, the feeling of a moral and political womb in which one feels safe when one sings along with other people – particularly when one is threatened by mighty social forces, reactionary forces. But, as I see it, it is an exception – a happy accident – when a song has this function, this wonderful function. There are few great songs which have done precisely that, or, to put it another way, there are few historical epochs that have produced such songs.

But there is another way of looking at how we listen to songs. (People in any case don't sing so much any more. The explosion of techniques for the reproduction of sound has, in a certain sense, made people dumb.) But on this level, too, songs have the effect of producing solidarity. The rulers, our reactionary rulers, always want to persuade the men and women whom they artificially isolate from each other, that they represent no political power, persuade them that they are alone, a forlorn hope in the war for freedom, as Heine calls it. And a song has also the function of a shout of encouragement: 'Hey, I'm here – we are still here – we are still alive – have still such and such hopes and expectations – we are doing this or that, can you help?' or else 'Watch out that nothing happens to you'. These are warning songs in which we give warning as birds do of a predator. There are songs to bring people together: 'Come with us.' There are all sorts, including sad songs, which have the interesting effect that they help people to discharge their political task of mourning, so that they can bear the mountain of sorrow, so that they are not overwhelmed by it. Sad songs cheer people up. Most folksongs are sad. That is not because ordinary people are a tear-sodden lot where their basic feelings are concerned. They are not cry-babies – but sad songs are good for making you feel happy. You get your sorrows off your back – you sing with a full throat and listen to what the throat has to say: that's another function of singing.

Protest songs? I think 'protest song' is a trendy expression. Admittedly I have not thought about it much, but if I turn it over in my mind, then I feel that I am not a 'protest' singer. I have a suspicion that it is a trendy word for a fashionable tendency. You see, the attitude of 'protest' has something pharisaical about it. The singer gives out bad marks – for what we already suspect to be a bad society, bad marks. If I am trying to make fun of the idea, I am not aiming my remarks at that protest which is contained in every political song, directly or indirectly. To hear that, of all things, from my mouth does sound a bit cheeky. For I am known precisely for the fact that my songs are critical.

I have a positive idea of society – I am, after all, a Communist, which doesn't say much these days because the most sharply opposed people call themselves that – but that is another story. And I do not consider myself to be someone who hands out bad marks on social conditions. A kind of poetical headmaster. But I do consider myself to be a man who stands in the midst of the political battles of his age, battles which are fierce for reasons quite unconnected with myself, and not because of the sharpness of my songs. Whatever harshness there is in my songs corresponds to the harshness of the class struggle in this world we live in. The harshness of the tone of my songs reflects nothing more or less than the harshness of the political confrontation between progress and reaction in our society. For in this non-capitalist society of ours, in the German Democratic Republic, which already calls itself – with some justification – socialist, we once more have progress and reaction. Of course that reaction is not bourgeois reaction, not those forces which wish for a return to bourgeois society. What we have is the reaction of monopolistic bureaucracy, which has been dubbed Stalinism – we have the computerised East bloc Stalinism, as I call it, and we have also – and this is all very crudely and simplistically put – the progressive forces, that is to say, those forces that want to achieve what, to use the slogan, is called 'socialist democracy', to fight for it and suffer for it. And that is another thing there are differences of opinion about.

When did I begin to sing? I began to sing under the Nazis. During these times my mother taught me all the Communist workers' songs. That's the first thing. Then she got it into my head that I wasn't allowed to sing them and – so far as my child's head could understand – she also taught me why I wasn't allowed to sing them. And I obeyed everything she taught me. I knew all the songs and sang them all – at home –

4

knowing that I was forbidden to sing them. So I always sang them in the morning from five to seven. That sounds odd but there was a very simple reason for it. My mother went to work in a factory – my father was in a concentration camp, in fact he was killed by the time 1942 came round. So I lay in bed for two hours alone and was frightened and sang. Then at seven my aunt fetched me to spend the day with her until my mother came home. And these two hours a day were, so to speak, my singing academy, my – what do you call it? – training sessions, my time for practice, my education as a singer.

My first public appearance as a singer took place about 1941. That was also both very funny and very sad. For once, my mother had got permission to visit my father. She travelled to Friesland with me. My father was in a concentration camp there – a camp where they dug peat for fuel. He was 'a moor-soldier'. There's a beautiful song about them. I remember the visit because it was naturally the great event of my childhood and I kept hearing about it. I don't know how far I still remember it myself or how far it is only reflected for the thousandth time through constant re-telling. That I can't say. However, we were allowed to see my father for a few minutes in a hut – in an office with a warder in uniform – and to sit opposite him. When my back was turned, my mother – with the permission of the warder – passed my father a bag of sweets so that my father could give them to me. I took the bag, gave my mother a sweet and then gave my father one and wanted, with a mechanical gesture, to give the man one too. Then I stopped and didn't want to give him one. My father smiled and said: 'Go on, give him one.' I thought about it for a little and then shut the bag and said 'No'. Then, wanting to please my father, my mother said to me: 'Sing something for your father.' And I sang – a very unpleasant song which I kept hearing on the radio: 'Bombs, bombs, over England'. And then I went 'Boom! Boom!', because that was part of this song too. Perhaps you can imagine my father's pleasure at seeing his small son and how desperately sad he must have been that his child was growing up with this Nazi ideology in his head. He didn't know I knew the other songs I had learned. It was naturally a matter of pure chance, brought about by necessity, and when people are sitting opposite each other for only a couple of minutes, then everything that happens in that couple of minutes acquires an exaggerated importance. When I think how hard, how bitter, it must have been for my father, how demoralising – well, it was a bad moment. But I didn't go on making this kind of appearance as a singer.

I came to the German Democratic Republic in 1953, at a time when the great tide was in the other direction – from East to West. I believe – after all I now know and all I have lived through – that this was the decisive step in my life, the first step I really made on my own responsibility. And it was the right one. In the West I would have been corrupted. Perhaps in a very pleasant way, as I can imagine. I would certainly have been able to exploit my so-called talent in some way or another, or let it be exploited, I should say. But corrupted I would have been one way or the other. I would perhaps have become a party boss in the German Communist Party or a pop-singer. Neither of much use to society. But that sounds a little too spiteful. Let me look at the matter more positively. It was a great good fortune for me that I could live here in the German Democratic Republic because I could simply develop better here. Over there I would also have had the opportunity to learn, but inside me I was not ready to learn in the West. In the West I was in a bad mechanical confrontation with society. Here – particularly in the early years – I experienced a downright joyous, fervent unity with society. I was, as the romantic saying goes, at home in my fatherland, in my father's land, in the land for which my father fought and died. That was very good for me; but for this very same reason, because of this same political passion, I came into conflict with this same land.

These are only two sides of one and the same thing. A land one loves, a society in which one is passionately involved, one cannot help criticising. Children don't stay children; young people don't stay young; students don't stay students – you learn about things. Long years of laborious study of marxist literature means you can't help understanding a few things about Marx. Or applying the yardstick of the materialist concept of history to one's own history. Then one is involved – on a higher level this time, on a historical level – in confrontations with this wonderful society. And it is precisely the communist critique of these conditions that causes the greatest rage in my reactionary comrades, produces the greatest fear, the greatest hatred; but it is nothing new in human history, after all, that people who have different views on the same course to be followed hate each other the most bitterly and, if they have the power, destroy each other.

Marx had the idea that we were gradually approaching a time when this barbaric law, together with the law of the exploitation of man by man, in which what I have described is the ideological and political reflection, might be over, because such exploitation is no longer necessary; nor is all the barbarity of man to man which derives from it in order precisely to maintain this exploitation of one human being by another – spiritually, materially, by police methods.

We are standing on the brink of such a society. It is all much more complicated, more tedious, than we had suspected and, by and large, the successful solution of this great social problem – whether man, as Marx says, builds a socialist or communist society or falls into barbarism – this battle is by no means won. That is why we cannot be complacent. I do not believe that marxism is invincible because it is true. That is one of the most stupid, most fatalistic, and most un-marxist solutions that we have produced here in our country, in our countries. Truth can certainly be defeated, if – to follow through with the image – the lie is well enough armed. And when even truth is used by the liars as a weapon, then the whole problem is made immensely more complicated.

This battle is by no means decided and we cannot allow ourselves much time. Hence this impatience, this feeling of unrest, which finds expression in my poems, because we do not have very much more time in which to tidy up our affairs. For mankind has only a little more time to solve the problems which the bourgeois scientists have totted up with their computers – all that talk about the environment, about the earth's supplies of energy, and of how man is approaching the extreme limits of our planet. These are all problems which I believe only a socialist society can solve. And we do not have very much more time to solve these problems, and if we do not solve them soon then they will no longer exist but that will come about in a way that will not be very pleasant for us. For even this great problem is precious – it will not be there much longer. Hence the impatience which appears so exaggerated to many people who have settled down comfortably in their misery, so annoying.

Wolf Biermann, an appreciation

> Oh friend, don't you feel the same way too?
> I can only love
>   what I am also free
>   to leave:
>
> this country
> this city
> this woman
> this life
>
> And it's just for that reason
> few love a country
> some a city
> many a woman
> yet all love life.
>   Biermann, *Mit Marx- und Engelszungen*

In 1971 the German magazine *Der Spiegel* published an interview with Wolf Biermann in which he defined his status as follows: 'You know that I am not allowed to make public appearances or publish in the German Democratic Republic because I have differences with my comrades who head the Party. These reactionary comrades are not intent on beating me to death, rather they silence me to death. They don't lock me up and keep me in our public life. They lock me out. My status here is so to speak that of a nationally recognised enemy of the state.'

In another interview in the same magazine two years later Biermann claimed that his greatest fear was that he might be forced to leave his country and adapt to the 'freedom' of the West. That would be the end for him. In fact, he might even stop writing.

Biermann's worst fear became a reality on 16 November 1976: the East German government informed Biermann, who had just begun a concert tour in West Germany, that he no longer was a citizen of the German Democratic Republic due to the slanderous remarks which he made about GDR 'socialism' during his first singing engagement. According to the GDR party and state leadership, Biermann could not be allowed to return to his country because of his anti-communist position.

Biermann did not react violently. In his first major interview after the forced exile, printed in the *Spiegel* again, he remarked: 'It makes a difference whether one is living in the GDR and utters critical remarks about GDR problems or whether one is living in the capitalist West – which I regard as reactionary. As a political artist, I'd be stupid if I did not take this into account. Certainly the so-called specialists in this area will have realized that my current political statements about GDR socialism are different from those which I had formerly made through interviews and writings. Never have I been more clear and passionate as I am now in my arguments about the vital nature and significance of the experiment which the GDR represents. Vital and important for all of Germany and the workers' movement in Germany.' Moreover, Biermann has tried to clarify why he still wants to return to the German Democratic Republic: 'Because this society with all its tumours is my society in which I live, which I know, in whose process I involve myself, which furthermore is conducting an experiment that one has dubbed with the slogan "socialism", an experiment which, I believe, all humanity must undergo if it does not want to degenerate into barbarism.'

It seems highly unlikely that Biermann will be allowed to return to the German Democratic Republic in the near future. But one thing is certain: Biermann will have to work through the major contradiction of his life. Adamant in his conviction that communism must be developed in countries like the German Democratic Republic and that this development is decisive for the potential success of a socialist movement in the West, Biermann is caught in the contradictory position of being persecuted for defending the cause which his own country claims to espouse.

Biermann's early childhood was marked by troubles much more grim. During the 1940s his father, who was Jewish and worked as a communist resistance fighter on the docks of Hamburg, was killed in Auschwitz. His mother, also in the Communist Party, managed to fend for Biermann. They both managed to survive the Nazi period. After the war Biermann attended school in Hamburg until 1953. Realising that the chances for developing as a communist in West Germany were extremely limited and wanting to demonstrate his sympathy with the GDR, he moved to East Berlin after the ill-fated workers' uprisings of June 1953 when thousands of East Germans were moving west. In East Berlin he began to study philosophy, economics, and mathematics. Most important was his early contact with Bertolt Brecht and Hanns Eisler at the Berliner Ensemble, where he worked as an assistant director. While working in the theatre, Biermann began to write his own songs and music, and he gradually built a reputation in the early 1960s as poet and ballad singer, whose terse sarcastic verses combined marxist analysis with penetrating political criticism of the social conditions in both East and West Germany.

As Biermann learned more about his 'adopted' country, he ran into difficulties, for he had never taken lessons in diplomacy. In 1962 he was prohibited from performing in public because of his criticism of the East German government's policies. This ban was just a warning and lasted a year. In 1964 he was allowed to make a concert tour of West Germany, where he sang his ballads and political songs and was hailed as the leading young poet of East Germany. After his return to East Berlin, he continued to perform even though his works were not permitted to appear in print and are still not available there. In December 1965, Biermann was once again attacked by the Sozialistische Einheitspartei (SED, Socialist Unity Party) for not adhering to East Germany's cultural policy, and since then he has not been allowed to perform officially in East Germany. The reasons for the SED's campaign against Biermann concern his 'bestial and frivolous' attacks on the party, which he allegedly slandered. Furthermore, he was accused of manifesting anarchistic and petty bourgeois attitudes in his poems, which are also considered to be antagonistic to socialism as the state sees it because they are filled with scepticism and cynicism.

If his critics continue to attack him as some sort of a revisionist or enemy of communism, then Biermann insists that they look more closely at the social conditions in the GDR to learn who the real enemy of the people and communism is – the state and party leadership which, he claims, uses him as a scapegoat. The basis for his disagreement with the state and party leadership concerns freedom and self-determination by the people in a socialist society which should be moving to do away with privileges and class distinctions. Biermann argues that the SED is more concerned with preserving its power and control from above than with initiating and completing socialist changes. His attempts as a communist writer are geared to present social concerns and seeing problems from the people's perspective. His early verse in *Die Drahtharfe* (1965, *The Wire Harp*, included here) clearly reveals both his critique of capitalism as well as his disappointment in the lack of revolutionary verve in the German Democratic Republic. As an East German, Biermann is primarily interested in working out problems faced by the people in his own society. His poems and ballads in *Mit Marx- und Engelszungen* (1968, *With the Tongues of Marx and Engels*) and *Für meine Genossen* (1972, *For My Comrades*) are aimed at showing his solidarity with genuine socialist comrades in their struggle against the more bureaucratic and technocratic members of the state and party leadership, whom he calls revisionist because they actually want to prevent the socialist revolution from being completed. Such poems and ballads as 'Genossen, wer von uns wäre nicht gegen den Krieg', 'Brecht, deine Nachgeborenen', and 'Vier sehr verschiedene Versuche mit den Genossen' are frontal attacks against members of the party, who have watered down the meaning of socialism and communism in order to establish themselves in control of the state.

Biermann's poetry is stamped in the tradition of Villon, Heine and Brecht, all of whom figure prominently in his verse. Commenting on his relationship to this tradition, Biermann has remarked: 'I believe that Erich Kuby is right when he says that Heinrich Heine's achievement consisted in his speaking the language of German classicism as though it were already folk language. This is similar to my method in using the language of the classicist Brecht.' It is not only Biermann's attempt to speak in the language of the people which is important, but his original use of music which he composes *against* the text. Biermann maintains that the music should not be a mere vehicle for carrying the text. The music attacks the lyrics which make an incomplete statement about the subject matter being treated, and in this sense, the music serves as a critique of the text. This antithetical tension in Biermann's ballads and poems which allows for abrupt changes of mood is necessary since he often writes about his personal problems, and he consciously uses the music and text to achieve an ironical stance. Whereas his irony prevents him from sinking into self-pity, it also allows him to project his personal situation objectively as representing that of young, serious comrades who seek to overcome the obstacles which slow down progress in East Germany. Incidentally, this is why his forced exile caused waves of protest in East Germany, not only by intellectuals but by workers.

Most of Biermann's themes are brought together in his only musical play thus far, *Der Dra-Dra* (1970), a witty communist fairy tale about Hans Folk, who arrives in a city to free the people from the despotic dragon Dra-Dra. There he learns that the people have become so depoliticized that they refuse to side with him. Hans has to rely on the animals (the lowest elements of the society) to bring about the revolution. Biermann cleverly uses tenets from Mao Tse-tung's philosophy and applies them to the realities in the German Democratic Republic. The play, which has never been performed in East Germany, caused a national scandal in West Germany, not so much because of the production itself, but because the director and actors in Munich wanted to publish a theatre programme that portrayed the local political 'dragons' as the oppressors of the people in West Germany.

Biermann's writings, which he often calls 'Hetzlieder' (provocative songs), tend to provoke the ire of the establishment, no matter where they are read or performed. He has focused on the record industry in the West as a means for making his communist position known and supporting international revolutionary movements. His last three records, *Aah-ja!* (1974), *Liebeslieder* (1975) and *Es gibt ein Leben vor dem Tod* (1976), amply document his own revolutionary intentions. Moreover, Biermann encourages people to make copies of his songs and verse so that they can be circulated privately in the East and contribute in some small way to the awakening of a socialist political consciousness, uncontaminated by the state. In one of his more recent books, *Deutschland, Ein Wintermärchen* (1973, *Germany, A Winter's Tale*), a parody of Heine's *A Winter's Tale*, he reaffirms his combative position. He ends

14

the long narrative by proclaiming that he will continue to sing for peace in the middle of war, and in the middle of peace he will sing for war, that is, for a revolutionary war against all those who have betrayed the socialist revolution.

Jack Zipes
Milwaukee, 1977

Portrait eines alten Mannes

Seht, Genossen, diesen Weltveränderer: Die Welt
Er hat sie verändert, nicht aber sich selbst
Seine Werke, sie sind am Ziel, er aber ist am Ende

Ist dieser nicht wie der Ochse im Joch
des chinesischen Rades? Die Wasser
hat er geschöpft. Die Felder
hat er gesättigt. Der Reis
grünt. Also schreitet dieser
voran im Kreise
und sieht auch vor sich nichts, als
abertausendmal eigene Spur im Lehm
Jahr für Jahr wähnt er also, der Einsame
den Weg zu gehen der Massen. Und er läuft doch
sich selbst nur nach. Sich selber nur
trifft er und findet sich nicht
und bleibt sich selber immer der Fernste

Seht, Genossen, diesen Weltveränderer: Die Welt
Er hat sie verändert, nicht aber sich selbst
Seine Werke, sie sind am Ziel, er aber ist am Ende

Das seht, Genossen. Und zittert!

Portrait of an old man

Look, comrades, at this world-changer: he has
changed the world all right, but not himself
His works have achieved their aim, but he is done for

Is this man not like the ox in the yoke
of the chinese wheel? He has
drawn the waters. He has
nourished the fields. The rice
grows green. And so this man
strides on in his circle
seeing nothing ahead of him but
his own tracks in the mud a thousand times over
So year after year, alone, he imagines
he's going the way of the masses. All the while
running after his own tail. It's only ever
himself he meets and never himself he finds
and always himself he remains farthest from

Look, comrades, at this world-changer: he has
Changed the world all right, but not himself
His works have achieved their aim, but he is done for

See that, comrades. And shiver.

Größe des Menschen

Nimm nur die Berge, die abträgt der Regen
und schwemmt sie flußwärts ins Meer wie nichts

Oder das Meer selber, das schiffemordende
in der Sturmflut, wie es die Inseln wegleckt

Oder wenn aufbrechen die Wunden der Erde
in Vulkanen, städtebegrabenden Massen

Oder auch, von denen wir wieder hörten:
den länderzertrümmernden Erdbeben

– sie alle übertrifft der Mensch
                in seiner Zerstörungskraft

Man's grandeur

Take mountains: rain carries them off and currents
wash them into the sea just like that

Or the sea itself, murdering ships
in tidal-waves, licking islands away

Or when the wounds of the earth break open
in volcanoes, masses burying cities

Or even, as we heard again the other day:
earthquakes laying whole countries to waste

– all these mankind outstrips
                    in his power to destroy

Frage und Antwort und Frage

Es heißt: Man kann nicht mitten im Fluß
die Pferde wechseln
Gut. Aber die alten sind schon ertrunken

Du sagst: Das Eingeständnis unserer Fehler
nütze dem Feind
Gut. Aber wem nützt unsere Lüge?

Manche sagen: Auf die Dauer ist der Sozialismus
gar nicht vermeidbar
Gut. Aber wer setzt ihn durch?

Question and answer and question

They say: you can't change horses
in mid-stream
True. But the old guard have drowned already

You say: admitting our faults
helps the enemy
True. But who do our lies help?

Many say: in the long run socialism
is inevitable
True. But who's going to make it happen?

Kleinstadtsonntag

Gehn wir mal hin?
Ja, wir gehn mal hin.
Ist hier was los?
Nein, es ist nichts los.
Herr Ober, ein Bier!
Leer ist es hier.
Der Sommer ist kalt.
Man wird auch alt.
Bei Rose gabs Kalb.
Jetzt isses schon halb.
Jetzt gehn wir mal hin.
Ja, wir gehn mal hin.
Ist er schon drin?
Er ist schon drin.
Gehn wir mal rein?
Na gehn wir mal rein.
Siehst du heut fern?
Ja, ich sehe heut fern.
Spielen sie was?
Ja, sie spielen was.
Hast du noch Geld?
Ja, ich habe noch Geld.
Trinken wir ein'?
Ja, einen klein'.
Gehn wir mal hin?
Ja, gehn wir mal hin.
Siehst du heut fern?

Ja   ich   sehe   heut   fern.

Small-town Sunday

Well, shall we go?
Yeh come on, let's go.
Any action round here?
No, no action round here.
Barman, a beer!
It's dead in here.
This summer's been cold.
And we're getting old.
Kate's did a roast.
Here, it's nearly half past.
Come on then, let's go.
Yeh come on, let's go.
Is he in tonight?
Yeh, he's in tonight.
Shall we go in?
OK, let's go in.
Watching telly tonight?
Yeh, it's my telly night.
Anything on?
Yeh, there's something on.
Got any cash?
Yeh, I got some cash.
Fancy a half?
Yeh well, just a half.
Well, shall we go?
Yeh come on, let's go.
Watching telly tonight?

Yeh, it's   my   telly   night.

Herr Brecht

Drei Jahre nach seinem Tode
ging Herr Brecht
Vom Hugenotten-Friedhof
die Friedrichstraße entlang,
zu seinem Theater.

Auf dem Wege traf er
einen dicken Mann
zwei dicke Fraun
einen Jungen.
Was, dachte er,
das sind doch die Fleißigen
vom Brechtarchiv.
Was, dachte er,
seid ihr immer noch nicht fertig
mit dem Ramsch?

Und er lächelte
unverschämt – bescheiden und
war zufrieden.

Herr Brecht

Three years after his death
Herr Brecht went
from the Huguenot Graveyard
along the Friedrichstrasse
to his theatre.

On his way he met
a fat man
two fat women
and a boy.
Well well, he thought,
that's that keen lot
from the Brecht archives.
Well well, he thought,
are they still sorting out
all that mess?

And he smiled his
insolent-modest smile
and was content.

Brigitte

Ich ging zu dir
dein Bett war leer.
Ich wollte lesen.
und dachte an nichts.
Ich wollte ins Kino
und kannte den Film.
Ich ging in die Kneipe
und war allein.
Ich hatte Hunger
und trank zwei Spezi.
Ich wollte allein sein
und war zwischen Menschen.
Ich wollte atmen
und sah nicht den Ausgang.
Ich sah eine Frau
die ist öfters hier.
Ich sah einen Mann
der stierte ins Bier.
Ich sah zwei Hunde
die waren so frei.
Ich sah auch die Menschen
die lachten dabei.
Ich sah einen Mann
der fiel in den Schnee
er war besoffen
es tat ihm nicht weh.
Ich rannte vor Kälte
über das Eis
der Straßen zu dir
die all das nicht weiß.

Brigitte

I went to you
your bed was empty.
I tried to read
and couldn't think.
I fancied the pictures
and had seen the film.
I went round the pub
and sat on my own.
I felt a bit hungry
and drank two specials.
I wanted to be alone
and was amongst people.
I wanted to breathe
and couldn't find the way out.
I saw a woman
she's often here.
I saw a man
staring into his beer.
I saw two dogs
they suited themselves.
I saw people too
laughing at them.
I saw a man
he fell in the snow
drunk as a lord
he didn't even know.
I ran to keep warm
across the ice
on the roads to you
who don't know all this.

Warte nicht auf beßre
Zeiten

Manchen hör ich bitter sagen
> Sozialismus – schön und gut
Aber was man uns hier aufsetzt
Das ist der falsche Hut! <
Manchen seh ich Fäuste ballen
In der tiefen Manteltasche
Kalte Kippen auf den Lippen
Und in den Herzen Asche

    Wartest du auf beßre Zeiten
    Wartest du mit deinem Mut
    Gleich dem Tor, der Tag für Tag
    An des Flusses Ufer wartet
    Bis die Wasser abgeflossen
    Die doch ewig fließen

Manche raufen sich die Haare
Manche seh ich haßerfüllt
Manche seh ich in das Wolltuch
des Schweigens eingehüllt
Manche hör ich abends jammern
> Was bringt uns der nächste Tag
An was solln wir uns noch klammern
An was? An was? An was? <

    Wartest du auf beßre Zeiten . . .

Manche hoffen, daß des Flusses
Wasser nicht mehr fließen kann
Doch im Frühjahr, wenn das Eis taut

Don't keep waiting for the good times

I hear a lot of people saying
'Socialism – well, all right
But what they're pulling on us here
it isn't worth a light!'
I see a lot of people clenching
buried fists in mackintoshes
Dog-ends hang cold from their lips
And in their hearts are ashes

> Are you waiting for the good times
> Are you saving up your spunk
> Like the fool who every day
> Stands beside the river waiting
> Thinking it will flow away
> But still it goes on flowing

Lots of people tear their hair out
I've seen plenty full of hate
I've seen plenty wrapped in silence
like a muffler round the throat
I've heard plenty moan come evening
'God, what will tomorrow bring?
There must be something to hold on to
Must be something, something, some thing.'

> Are you waiting for the good times . . .

Lots of people hope the river's
waters never flow again
But in springtime when the ice thaws

fängt es erst richtig an
Manche wollen diese Zeiten
wie den Winter überstehn
Doch wir müssen Schwierigkeiten
Bestehn! Bestehn! Bestehn –

    Warte nicht auf beßre Zeiten
    Warte nicht mit deinem Mut . . .

Viele werden dafür sorgen
daß der Sozialismus siegt
Heute! Heute, nicht erst morgen!
Freiheit kommt nie verfrüht
Und das beste Mittel gegen
Sozialismus (sag ich laut)
ist, daß ihr den Sozialismus
AUFBAUT!!! Aufbaut! (aufbaut)

    Wartet nicht auf beßre Zeiten
    Wartet nicht mit eurem Mut
    Gleich dem Tor, der Tag für Tag
    An des Flusses Ufer wartet
    Bis die Wasser abgeflossen
    Die doch ewig fließen
      die doch ewig fließen

then it starts and only then
Lots of people want to see out
these days as you would the winter
but we have to face up to them
Face up! Face up! Face up –

> Don't keep waiting for the good times
> Don't keep saving up your spunk . . .

Lots of people will make sure that
socialism triumphs here
Now! Today and not tomorrow!
Freedom's time's too dear
And the best of weapons against
socialism (I say out loud)
is that to get socialism
you *BUILD* it!!! Build it! (build it) '

> Don't keep waiting for the good times
> Don't keep saving up your spunk
> Like the fool who every day
> Stands beside the river waiting
> Thinking it will flow away
> But still it goes on flowing
>   still it goes on flowing

Berlin

Berlin, du deutsche deutsche Frau
Ich bin dein Hochzeitsfreier
Ach, deine Hände sind so rauh
von Kälte und von Feuer.

Ach, deine Hüften sind so schmal
wie deine schmalen Straßen
Ach, deine Küsse sind so schal,
ich kann dich nimmer lassen.

Ich kann nicht weg mehr von dir gehn
Im Westen steht die Mauer
Im Osten meine Freunde stehn,
der Nordwind ist ein rauher.

Berlin, du blonde blonde Frau
Ich bin dein kühler Freier
dein Himmel ist so hunde-blau
darin hängt meine Leier.

Berlin

Berlin, you oh so German lass
I court you with desire
But oh, your hands are rough, alas
from cold winds and from fire.

And oh, so narrow are your hips
just like your streets so narrow
And oh, so tepid are your lips
I know I'll never leave you.

I can no longer leave you now
The wall is to the west
And to the east I have my friends
the north wind is the harshest.

Berlin, the oh so blonde-haired lass
I court with cool desire
Your sky is such a lousy blue
And there I hang my lyre.

Spielzeug

Mit der Eisenbahn
lernen wir
zur Oma fahrn.
Das macht Spaß
Mit der Puppe
essen wir
gerne unsere Suppe
Das macht Spaß
Mit dem Ball
schmeißen wir
Peters Bären um
der ist dumm
Mit den Muschikatzen
lernt der Paul
die Anne kratzen
Das macht Spaß
Mit dem Panzer lernen wir:
Wie man
Eisenbahn,
Puppe, Suppe,
Ball und Bär,
Muschikatzen
und noch mehr
Anne, Pappa,
Haus und Maus
einfach kaputt macht.

Toys

With our choo-choo train
we learn
to go to Gran's again.
That is fun
With our dolly
eating soup
is much more jolly
That is fun
With our ball
we make
Peter's teddy fall
he's a fool
With our pussy-cat
Paul learns
to give Anne a scratch
That is fun
With our tanks we learn
how
choo-choo
jolly dolly
ball and bear,
pussy-cat
and much besides
Annie, Daddy,
house and mouse
get smashed to pieces.

Ballade von der beißwütigen Barbara

Sie hat mich beim Küssen gebissen aufs Blut
Sie biß mir nicht nur den Mund.

Und wie ich auch schrie – da lachte sie nur.
So kam ich
            auf den Hund.

Ich briet ihr ein Beefsteak mit Pfeffer und Salz
Für ihren beißgierigen Zahn.

Sie lachte und schmiß es zum Fenster 'raus
Und küßte
            und biß mich dann.

Ich war auf ihr Rad geflochten wie
Ein armer Küsseklau.

Sie lachte ja nur und sie brach mir so wild
Die Glieder
            die schlimme Frau.

Es hatte mein armer geschundener Leib
Kein heiles Stück Haut und kein Fett.

Doch als ich ihr sagte: bye bye, mein Kind,
Da biß sie
            in ihr Bett.

Die Wunden sind lange ausgeheilt.
Mich liebt jetzt die sanfte Marie.

Ballad of biting-mad Barbara

She kissed me and bit me until the blood ran
She didn't just kiss my mouth.

And then when I yelled – she just simply laughed
And that's how
        I lost out.

I cooked her a fine steak with pepper and salt
For her tooth with its biting yen.

She laughed and she chucked it straight out the window
Then kissed me
        and bit me again.

My body was broken on her cruel rack
Just like a poor kissing fool.

But she simply laughed and just savagely crushed
My limbs,
        the naughty girl.

My poor old body so flayed and so sore
Was mostly bruised skin and bare bone.

But when the time came to say: wiedersehen
She bit into
        her pillow.

The wounds that she gave me have long since been healed
Now I'm loved by the gentle Marie.

Doch wenn ich Marie im Arme halt,
Dann denk ich
DANN DENK ICH
Dann denk ich

nicht an Marie.

But when I hold gentle Marie in my arms
I'm thinking
I'M THINKING
I'm thinking

not of Marie.

Soldat Soldat

1

Soldat Soldat in grauer Norm
Soldat Soldat in Uniform
Soldat Soldat, ihr seid so viel
Soldat Soldat, das ist kein Spiel
Soldat Soldat, ich finde nicht
Soldat Soldat, dein Angesicht
Soldaten sehn sich alle gleich
Lebendig und als Leich

2

Soldat Soldat, wo geht das hin
Soldat Soldat, wo ist der Sinn
Soldat Soldat, im nächsten Krieg
Soldat Soldat, gibt es kein Sieg
Soldat Soldat, die Welt ist jung
Soldat Soldat, so jung wie du
Die Welt hat einen tiefen Sprung
Soldat, am Rand stehst *du*

3

Soldat Soldat in grauer Norm
Soldat Soldat in Uniform
Soldat Soldat, ihr seid so viel
Soldat Soldat, das ist kein Spiel
Soldat Soldat, ich finde nicht
Soldat Soldat, dein Angesicht
Soldaten sehn sich alle gleich
Lebendig und als Leich

Soldaten sehn sich alle gleich
– lebendig und als Leich

Soldier soldier

1

Soldier soldier, a hollow form
Soldier soldier, in uniform
Soldier soldier, you're all the same
Soldier soldier, it's not a game
Soldier soldier, I cannot place
Soldier soldier, your unknown face
Soldiers are identical
The quick, the dead and all

2

Soldier soldier, where will it lead
Soldier soldier, please use your head
Soldier soldier, no-one will win
Soldier soldier, in war again
Soldier soldier, the world like you
Soldier soldier, is young and green
But now the world has split in two
And you stand in between

3

Soldier soldier, a hollow form
Soldier soldier, in uniform
Soldier soldier, you're all the same
Soldier soldier, it's not a game
Soldier soldier, I cannot place
Soldier soldier, your unknown face
Soldiers are identical
The quick, the dead and all

Soldiers are identical
– the quick, the dead and all

Von mir und meiner Dicken
in den Fichten

Bloß paar schnelle Sprünge weg vom Wege
Legte ich ihr weißes Fleisch ins Gras
Mittagsonne brannte durch die Fichten
Als ich sie mit meinem Maße maß
Käfer krochen unter uns, es brachen
Heere Ameisen froh in uns ein
Etwa zwischen Bauch und Bauch zu baden
Oder irren zwischen Bein und Bein

Horden Mücken soffen sich von Sinnen
Stachen mich, weil ich ja oben schwamm
Bis ein Wolkenbruch, ein schneller greller
Uns in seine guten Arme nahm
Traubenschwere Wassertropfen fielen
Faul herab auf unsre heiße Haut
Und der wundermilde Guß von oben
Hat den großen Tod uns nicht versaut

Als ich endlich flach lag auf dem Rücken
Kippten meine Augen müde hoch
Einen Düsenjäger sah ich schweben
Durch ein aufgebauschtes Wolkenloch
Schwebte hin, schrieb einen sanften Bogen
Bis hinunter in das hohe Blau
Wieder brach die Sonne durch die Fichten
Und wir dampften im Nachmittagstau

On me and my pud in the
woods

Just two quick steps off the straight and narrow
In the grass I laid her white flesh down
As the mid-day sun shone through the pine-trees
My head found the measure of her crown
Beetles crept beneath us, squads of ants came
To invade us gaily as we lay
Either bathing in between our bellies
Or between our limbs to blindly stray

Hordes of midges drank themselves unconscious
And because I swam on top, stung me
Then a cloudburst, swift and glaring, saved us
Took us in its arms protectively
Lazily upon our heated skins then
Drops like heavy grapes began to fall
And this gentle miracle above us
Didn't spoil our happy end at all

When at last I lay back flat and drowsing
Tipped my tired eyes up to the sky
So I saw a jet-plane swiftly swinging
Through a puffed-up cloud-hole in the sky
Swing on down and draw a silent circle
Right on through below into the blue
Then the sun broke once more through the pine-trees
And we steamed in our afternoon dew

Bilanzballade im dreißigsten Jahr

Nun bin ich dreißig Jahre alt
Und ohne Lebensunterhalt
Und hab an Lehrgeld schwer bezahlt
Und Federn viel gelassen
Frühzeitig hat man mich geehrt
Nachttöpfe auf mir ausgeleert
Die Dornenkrone mir verehrt
Ich hab sie liegen lassen
    Und doch: Die Hundeblume blüht
    Auch in der Regenpfütze
    Noch lachen wir
    Noch machen wir nur Witze

Warum hat mich mein Vater bloß
Mit diesem folgenschweren Stoß
Gepflanzt in meiner Mutter Schoß
– Vielleicht, damit ich später
Der deutschen Bürokratensau
Balladen vor den Rüssel hau
Auf rosarote Pfoten hau
Die fetten Landesväter
    Und doch: Die Hundeblume blüht . . .

Ich hab mich also eingemischt
In Politik, das nützte nischt
Sie haben mich vom Tisch gewischt
Wie eine Mücke
Und als ich sie in' Finger stach
Und mir dabei den Stachel brach
Zerrieben sie mich ganz gemach
In kleine Stücke
    Und doch: Die Hundeblume blüht . . .

Balance-sheet ballad at thirty

Now that I'm thirty years of age
I'm still without a steady wage
It's cost a lot to be a sage
A lot of fur has flown
Before my time they honoured me
They poured their piss-pots over me
And put their crown of thorns on me
I left those things alone
    But still the dandelion blooms
    Though even in a puddle
    And still we laugh
    Still just make jokes of it all

Now why the hell my father chose
To plant the fateful seed that rose
Within my mother's lap, God knows
– Perhaps so that much later
I'd come to chuck my ballads at
The snouts of German bureaucrats
And tip our country's chiefs so fat
Up on their rosy trotters
    But still the dandelion blooms . . .

So into politics I roared
But even then it did no good
They simply swept me from the board
Just like little nits
And when I stung them in the finger
And in the process lost my stinger
They coolly ground this hapless singer
Into little bits
    But still the dandelion blooms . . .

Dies Deutschland ist ein Rattennest
Mein Freund, wenn du dich kaufen läßt
Egal, für Ostgeld oder West
Du wirst gefressen
Und während man noch an dir kaut
Dich schlecht bezahlt und gut verdaut
Bevor der nächste Morgen graut
Bist du vergessen
        Und doch: Die Hundeblume blüht...

Ich segelte mit steifem Mast
Zu mancher Schönen, machte Rast
Und hab die andern dann verpaßt
Es gibt zu viele
Jetzt hat mein schönes Boot ein Leck
Die Planken faulen langsam weg
Es tummeln sich, ich seh mit Schreck
Die Haie unterm Kiele
        Und doch: Die Hundeblume blüht...

Die Zeit hat ungeheuren Schwung
Paar Jahre bist du stark und jung
Dann sackst du langsam auf den Grund
Der Weltgeschichte
So manche Generation
Lief Sturm auf der Despoten Thron
Und wurd beschissen um den Lohn
Und ward zunichte

        Und doch: Die Freiheitsblume blüht
        Auch in der Regenpfütze
        Noch lachen wir
        Noch machen wir nur Witze

            Und doch: Die Hundeblume blüht
            Auch in der Regenpfütze
            Noch lachen wir.

My friend, this Germany's a nest
Of rats both in the East and West
And once you sell yourself you're just
Rats' fodder
And while they gnaw on at your bones
Digest you whole and pay you crumbs
Before the next day's dawning comes
You'll be forgotten
      But still the dandelion blooms . . .

I sailed on with my mast erect
Found many a beauty, had the best
And then of course I missed the rest
The field's colossal
And now my good ship's sprung a leak
The deck-joints have begun to creak
I see with dread sharks' tail-fins peak
Below my vessel
      But still the dandelion blooms . . .

Our time goes at a fearful pace
A few years full of youth and grace
And then you fall flat on your face
Before world history
For men have time and time again
Waged war against the despot's reign
And then been shat on for their pain
And been destroyed

      But still the freedom-flower blooms
      Though even in a puddle
      And still we laugh
      Still just make jokes of it all

      But still the dandelion blooms
      Though even in a puddle
      And still we laugh.

Großes Gebet der
alten Kommunistin Oma Meume
in Hamburg

1

GOtt, lieber Gott im Himml, hör mich betn
Zu Dir schrei ich wie in der Kinderzeit
Warum hat mich mein armer Vater nicht zertretn
Als ich noch selig schlief in Mutters Leib
Nun bin ich alt, ein graues taubes Weib
Mein kurzes Leben lang war reichlich Not
Viel Kampf mein Gott, viel für das bißchen Brot
Nach Friedn schrie ich in die großn Kriege
Und was hab ich erreicht? Bald bin ich tot
O GOtt, laß DU den Kommunismus siegn!

2

Gott, glaube mir: Nie wird der Mensch das schaffn
Ich hab mich krumm gelegt für die Partei
Erinner Dich, wie ich Karl Scholz mit Waffn
Bei mir versteckt hab und bekocht dabei!
Auf Arbeit Tag für Tag die Schinderei
Dann dieser Hitler, das vergeß ich nie
Wie brach unsre Partei da in die Knie
Die Bestn starbn im KZ wie Fliegn
Die Andern sind verreckt im Krieg wie Vieh
O GOtt, laß DU den Kommunismus siegn!

3

Mensch, Gott! Wär uns bloß *der* erspart gebliebn
Der Stalin, meintwegen durch ein Attntat
Gott, dieser Teufel hat es fast getriebn
– verzeih – wie ein Faschist im Sowjetstaat
Und war doch selber Kommunist und hat

48

The old communist
Grandma Meume's Great Prayer
in Hamburg

1

GOd, dear God in Heaven, hear me praying
I call you now as when I was a kid
Why did my poor old father not destroy me
While in my mother's womb I still lay hid
Now that I'm old, a grey and deaf old woman
The whole of my short life was plagued with need
A lot of struggle, God, just for a little bread
I strained my voice for peace in two great wars
And what did I achieve? Soon I'll be dead
O GOd, can't YOU make communism triumph?!

2

God, believe me, man will never do it
I've bent my back to serve the party's good
Remember how I hid Karl Scholz at my place
His guns and all, and even cooked his food
I've grafted day by day for the oppressor
And then that Hitler, him I won't forget
How then our party broke down on its knees
The best all died in concentration camps
The others snuffed it in the war like fleas
O GOd, can't YOU make communism triumph?!

3

Christ, God, if we'd only been spared Stalin
To my mind there was one to assassinate
God, that bastard carried on – forgive me –
Almost like a fascist in a soviet state
And yet he was a communist himself

Millionen Kommunisten umgebracht
Und hat das Volk geknecht mit all die Macht
Und log das Aas, daß sich die Balkn biegn
Was hat der Hund uns aufn Hund gebracht
O GOtt, laß DU den Kommunismus siegn!

4
STOSSGEBET
Mach, daß mein herznslieber Wolf nicht endet
Wie schon sein Vater hinter Stachldraht!
Mach, daß sein wirrer Sinn sich wieder wendet
Zu der Partei, die ihn verstoßn hat
Und mach mir drüben unsern Friednsstaat
So reich und frei, daß kein Schwein mehr abhaut
Und wird dann auch die Mauer abgebaut
Kann Oma Meume selig auf zum Himml fliegn
Sie hat ja nicht umsonst auf Dich gebaut
Dann, lieber Gott, wird auch der Kommunismus siegn!

But still put tons of communists to death
And put the screws on people with his might
And lied, the sod, until the roof fell in
The pig, he really had us on all right
O GOd, can't YOU make communism triumph?!

4
FINAL PRAYER
God, please see my dearest Wolf don't end up
Like his father did behind barbed wire
See his wayward mind is quickly reconciled
To the party which went and kicked him out
And for my sake please make it over there
That peaceful state we want that's rich and free
So that no bugger hops the wall and then
They can pull it down and I'll die happy
To know I didn't trust in you in vain
Dear God, 'cos only then will communism triumph!

Die Ballade von dem Drainage-Leger
Fredi Rohsmeisl aus Buckow

1

Das ist die Ballade von Fredi Rohsmeisl
Drainage-Leger auf den Äckern um Buckow
Gummistiefel hoch bis zum Bauch
Sein Häuschen links am Fischerkietz.
Bei Lene Kutschinsky war Tanz
Er hat auseinander getanzt
Mit seiner Verlobten – das war verboten
Na schön . . .

    Junge, ich hab Leube schon tanzen sehn
    Junge, das war manchmal schon nicht mehr schön.
    Aber schadet uns das?
    Nein.

2

Und als er so wild auseinander tanzt
Die Musik war heiß und das Bier war warm
Da hatten ihn plötzlich zwei Kerle am Arm
Und schmissen ihn auf die Taubengasse.
Und schmissen ihn über den Lattenzaun
Und haben ihn in die Fresse gehaun
Und er hatte noch nichts getan
Und hatte den hellblauen Anzug an.

    Junge, ich hab Leute schon schlagen sehn
    Junge, das war manchmal schon nicht mehr schön.
    Aber nützt uns das?
    Nein.

The ballad of Freddy Rohsmeisl, drainage-layer from Buckow

1

This is the ballad of Freddy Rohsmeisl
Drainage-layer from the farmland near Buckow
Wellington boots right up to his navel
His house on the left by the Fischerkietz.
At Lena Kutschinsky's they had a dance
Freddy got up and started to dance
Apart, with his sweetheart
– not allowed. Yeh well . . .

> Look friend, I've seen people dance before
> Perhaps not the prettiest thing I ever saw
> But does it do any harm?
> No.

2

And while he was madly dancing apart
The music was hot and the beer was warm
Two blokes grabbed him suddenly by the arm
And chucked him out into the Taubengasse.
And chucked him over the wooden paling
And gave his kisser a proper pasting
And he hadn't done a blessed thing
In the best blue suit he was wearing.

> Look friend, I've seen people fight before
> Perhaps not the prettiest thing I ever saw
> But does it do any good?
> No.

3
Da hat Fredi Rohsmeisl beide verrammt
Zwei links zwei rechts er traf genau
Und waren zwei große Kerle die zwei
Halb Buckow sah ihm zu dabei.
Das Überfallauto kam antelefoniert
Hat Fredi halb tot gehaun
Das haben die Buckower Männer gesehn
Und auch die Buckower Fraun.

Junge, ich hab Leute schon zusehn sehn
Junge, das war manchmal schon nicht mehr schön.
Aber nützt uns das?
Nein.

4
Dann kriegte er einen Prozeß an Hals
Als Konterrevolutionär
Wo nahm der Staatsanwalt nur das Recht
Für zwölf Wochen Knast her?!
Seitdem frißt ihn ein stiller Zorn
Und nach dem zehnten Bier
Erzählt er Dir seine große Geschichte
Von hinten und auch von vorn.

Junge, ich hab Leute schon weinen sehn
Junge, das war manchmal schon nicht mehr schön.
Aber nützt uns das?
Nein.

5
Und er findet noch kein Ende
Und er ist voll Bitterkeit
Und er glaubt nicht einen Faden
Mehr an Gerechtigkeit.

3

Then Freddy Rohsmeisl turned on them both
The old one-two, he couldn't miss
And they were both big fellas, these two
Half Buckow stood by and watched all this.
The Flying Squad was there in a flash
Mangled Freddy black and blue
The men of Buckow stood by and watched
And the women of Buckow too.

> Look friend, I've seen people watch before
> Perhaps not the prettiest thing I ever saw
> But does it do any good?
> No.

4

So he got lumbered with a court case
As a counter-revolutionary
But where'd the prosecutor get the right
To land him with three months' solitary?
Since then he's simmered in silent rage
And after our Freddy's had a few
He'll tell you his story from beginning to end
And from end to beginning too.

> Look friend, I've seen people cry before
> Perhaps not the prettiest thing I ever saw
> But does it do any good?
> No.

5

And he can't see any end to it
And he's full of bitterness
And as for social justice
Well, he couldn't care less.

Er ist für den Sozialismus
Und für den neuen Staat
Aber den Staat in Buckow
Den hat er gründlich satt.

Junge, ich hab Leute schon fluchen sehn
Junge, das war manchmal schon nicht mehr schön.
Aber nützt uns das?
Nein!

6
Da gingen einige Jahre ins Land
Da gingen einige Reden ins Land
Da änderte sich allerhand
Daß mancher sich nicht wiederfand.
Und als der zehnte Sputnik flog
Da wurde heiß auseinander getanzt
Der Staatsanwalt war selbst so frei.
Und Fredi sah ihm zu dabei.

Junge, ich hab Leute sich ändern sehn
Junge, das war manchmal schoneinfach schön.
Aber nützt uns das? (Ja.)

He still believes in socialism
In the New State and all
But as for the new state in Buckow
He's had a bellyful.

> Look friend, I've seen people swear before
> Perhaps not the prettiest thing I ever saw
> But does it do any good?
> No!

6

A few years swept across the land
A few speeches swept across the land
Suddenly everything had changed
You didn't know your left from your right hand.
And the day the tenth sputnik flew in space
Everyone was dancing apart
Even the prosecutor didn't say no
And Freddy stood by and watched the show.

> Look friend, I've seen people change before
> Perhaps that was the prettiest thing I ever saw
> But does it do any good? (Yes.)

Ermutigung

Peter Huchel gewidmet

Du, laß dich nicht verhärten
In dieser harten Zeit
Die all zu hart sind, brechen
Die all zu spitz sind, stechen
und brechen ab sogleich

Du, laß dich nicht verbittern
In dieser bittren Zeit
Die Herrschenden erzittern
– sitzt du erst hinter Gittern –
Doch nicht vor deinem Leid

Du, laß dich nicht erschrecken
In dieser Schreckenszeit
Das wolln sie doch bezwecken
Daß wir die Waffen strecken
Schon vor dem großen Streit

Du, laß dich nicht verbrauchen
Gebrauche deine Zeit
Du kannst nicht untertauchen
Du brauchst uns, und wir brauchen
Grad deine Heiterkeit

Wir wolln es nicht verschweigen
In dieser Schweigezeit
Das Grün bricht aus den Zweigen
Wir wolln das allen zeigen
Dann wissen sie Bescheid

Encouragement

dedicated to Peter Huchel

Don't let yourself be hardened
In these hard times of ours
The hard ones break so easy
The sharp ones sting so easy
And then are dead in hours

Don't let yourself be bitter
In bitter times like ours
While in a cell you're sitting
The rulers will be fretting
Though not for you of course

Don't let yourself be frightened
Though these are frightening times
That's all they want, the bastards
That long before the fight starts
We offer up our arms

Don't let yourself be misused
Make full use of your hours
You can't just disappear now
You need us and we need somehow
That cheerfulness of yours

We'll make no secret of it
Our times may be obscure
But soon each branch will flower
There'll be no need to cower
And then they'll know for sure

Moritat auf Biermann seine
Oma Meume in Hamburg

Als meine Oma ein Baby war
Vor achtundachtzig Jahrn
Da ist ihre Mutter im Wochenbett
Mit Schwindsucht zum Himmel gefahrn
Als meine Oma ein Baby war
Ihr Vater war Maschinist
Bis gleich darauf die rechte Hand
Ihm abgerissen ist

Das war an einem Montag früh
Da riß die Hand ihm ab
Er war noch froh, daß die Fabrik
Den Wochenlohn ihm gab
Als meine Oma ein Baby war
Mit ihrem Vater allein
Da fing der Vater Saufen an
Und ließ das Baby schrein

Dann ging er in die Küche rein
Und auf den Küchenschrank
Da stellte er ganz oben rauf
Die kleine Küchenbank
Und auf die Bank zwei Koffer noch
Und auf den schiefen Turm
Ganz oben rauf aufs Federbett
Das kleine Unglückswurm

Dann ging er mit dem letzten Geld
In MEYERS FREUDENHAUS
Und spülte mit Pfefferminz-Absinth

Moritat for Biermann's
Grandma Meume in Hamburg

When my old Gran was just a babe
Eighty-eight years ago
Her mother got TB in labour
And to heaven she did go
When my old Gran was just a babe
Her father turned a machine
Until one day it turned on him
And took his hand off clean

It was a Monday morning when
His hand was whipped away
He thanked his lucky stars the firm
Gave him a full week's pay
When my old Gran was just a babe
She'd just her Dad, that's all
But then he took to boozing beer
And let the baby bawl

He went into the scullery
And on the cabinet
He put right at the very top
Their tiny kitchen seat
And on the seat two suit-cases
And on this wobbling castle
Lying on her featherbed
The poor unlucky parcel

Then off to MEYER'S PLEASURE-HOUSE
He took his last week's pay
And downing peppermint-absinth

Sich das Gewissen raus
Und kam zurück im Morgengraun
Besoffen und beschissen
Und stellte fest: >Verflucht, das Wurm
Hat sich nicht totgeschmissen!<

Das Kind lag friedlich da und schlief
Hoch oben auf dem Turm
Da packte er mit seiner Hand
Das kleine Unglückswurm
Nahm es behutsam in den Arm
Und weinte Rotz und Wasser
Und lallte ihm ein Wiegenlied
Vor Glück und Liebe fraß er

Der Oma fast ein Öhrchen ab
Und schwor, nie mehr zu trinken
Und weil er Maschinist gewesen war
Schwor er das mit der Linken
Das ist ein Menschenalter her
Hätt sie sich totgeschmissen
Dann würde ich von alledem
Wahrscheinlich garnix wissen

Die Alte lebt heut immer noch
Und kommst du mal nach Westen
Besuch sie mal und grüß sie schön
Vom Enkel, ihrem besten
Und wenn sie nach mir fragt und weint
Und auf die Mauer flucht
Dann sage ihr: Bevor sie stirbt
Wird sie noch mal besucht

Und während du von mir erzählst
Schmiert sie dir, erster Klasse

He washed his cares away
He came back at the break of day
With booze still on his breath
And cursed to see the kid had not
Fallen to her death

The child lay there in peace and slept
High up on that castle
So then with his one hand he grabbed
The poor unlucky parcel
He took her gently in his arms
And slobbering snot and water
He hummed to her a lullaby
Of love and joy to his daughter

He nearly chewed my Gran's ear off
He vowed to drink no more
He swore with his left hand because
He'd turned machines before
All this was many years ago
If she'd fallen then and there
I wouldn't now be here to sing
About the whole affair

The old girl's still alive today
And if you're over in the West
Look her up and wish her from
Her grandson all the best
And if she asks about me, cries
And rages at The Wall
Please tell her that before she dies
I'll come and pay a call

And while you're telling her my news
She'll make you soup, none finer

Ein Schmalzbrot, dazu Muckefuck
In einer blauen Tasse
Vielleicht hat sie auch Lust, und sie
Erzählt dir paar Geschichten
Und wenn die schön sind, komm zurück
Die mußt du mir berichten

Bread and dripping too she'll do
All served on her best china
Perhaps the mood'll take her and
She'll tell a tale or two
And if they're good, when you get back
I'd like to hear them too

Die Ballade von dem Briefträger
William L. Moore aus Baltimore

der im Jahre 63 allein in die Südstaaten wanderte
Er protestierte gegen die Verfolgung der Neger.
Er wurde erschossen nach einer Woche.
Drei Kugeln trafen ihn in die Stirn.

SONNTAG

Sonntag, da ruhte William L. Moore
von seiner Arbeit aus.
Er war ein armer Briefträger nur,
in Baltimore stand sein Haus.

MONTAG

Montag, ein Tag in Baltimore,
sprach er zu seiner Frau:
> Ich will nicht länger Briefträger sein,
ich geh nach Süden auf Tour (that's sure) <
    BLACK AND WHITE, UNITE! UNITE!
    schrieb er auf ein Schild.
    White and black – die Schranken weg!
    Und er ging ganz allein.

DIENSTAG

Dienstag, ein Tag im Eisenbahnzug,
fragte William L. Moore
manch einer nach dem Schild, das er trug,
und wünscht ihm Glück für die Tour.
    BLACK AND WHITE, UNITE! UNITE!
    stand auf seinem Schild . . .

MITTWOCH

Mittwoch, in Alabama ein Tag,
ging er auf der Chaussee,

The ballad of postman
William L. Moore from Baltimore

who marched on his own into the Southern States in 1963.
He protested against the persecution of the negroes.
He was shot after a week.
Three bullets struck his forehead.

SUNDAY

Sunday meant rest for William L. Moore
after a hard week's work.
He was only a postman and pretty poor,
he came from Baltimore.

MONDAY

Monday, one day in Baltimore,
he said to Mrs Moore:
I don't want to be a postman no more,
I'm going down south on a tour.
>   BLACK AND WHITE, UNITE! UNITE!
>   on a placard he wrote.
>   *White and black – hold repression back!*
>   And he set off on his own.

TUESDAY

Tuesday, one day on the railway train,
people asked William L. Moore
what was the sign he was carrying,
and wished him luck for his tour.
>   BLACK AND WHITE, UNITE! UNITE!
>   stood on his placard . . .

WEDNESDAY

Wednesday, one day in Alabama,
walking down the main street,

weit war der Weg nach Birmingham,
taten die Füße ihm weh.
  BLACK AND WHITE, UNITE! UNITE!

DONNERSTAG
Donnerstag hielt der Sheriff ihn an,
sagte >Du bist doch weiß!<
Sagte >Was gehn die Nigger dich an?
Junge, bedenke den Preis!<
  BLACK AND WHITE, UNITE! UNITE!

FREITAG
Freitag lief ihm ein Hund hinterher,
wurde sein guter Freund.
Abends schon trafen Steine sie schwer –
sie gingen weiter zu zweit.
  BLACK AND WHITE, UNITE! UNITE!

SONNA'MT
Sonna'mt, ein Tag, war furchtbar heiß,
kam eine weiße Frau,
gab ihm ein'n Drink, und heimlich sprach sie:
>Ich denk wie Sie ganz genau.<
  BLACK AND WHITE, UNITE! UNITE!

LAST DAY
Sonntag, ein blauer Sommertag,
lag er im grünen Gras –
blühten drei rote Nelken blutrot
auf seiner Stirne, so blaß.
  BLACK AND WHITE, UNITE! UNITE!
  steht auf seinem Schild.
  White and black – die Schranken weg!
  Und er starb ganz allein.
  Und er bleibt nicht allein.

still a long way from Birmingham,
he'd already got aching feet.
    BLACK AND WHITE, UNITE! UNITE!

THURSDAY
Thursday, the day the sheriff stopped him,
said: 'What the hell – you're white!
What business of yours is the niggers, man?
If it's trouble you want – all right!'
    BLACK AND WHITE, UNITE! UNITE!

FRIDAY
Friday, a dog started following him,
became his only friend.
By evening stones were hitting them both,
but they went on to the end.
    BLACK AND WHITE, UNITE! UNITE!

SAT'DAY
Sat'day, that day it was terribly hot,
a white woman came up to the two,
gave him a drink and secretly whispered:
'I think the same as you.'
    BLACK AND WHITE, UNITE! UNITE!

LAST DAY
Sunday, a blue and summer's day,
he lay in the grass so green –
three red carnations blooming blood-red
on his forehead could be seen.
    BLACK AND WHITE, UNITE! UNITE!
    stood on his placard.
    White and black – hold repression back!
    And he died on his own.
    And he won't be alone.

Kunststück.

Wenn ich mal heiß bin
Wenn ich mal heiß bin
    lang ich mir ne Wolke runter
    und wring sie über mir aus.
Kalte Dusche.
             Kunststück.

Wenn ich mal kalt bin
Wenn ich mal kalt bin
    lang ich mir die Sonne runter
    und steck sie mir ins Jackett.
Kleiner Ofen.
             Kunststück.

Wenn ich bei ihr bin
Wenn ich bei ihr bin
    schwimmen Wolken mit uns runter
    rollt die Sonne gleich mit.
Das ist Liebe.
             Kunststück.

Wenn ich mal müd bin
Wenn ich mal müd bin
    lang ich mir den lieben Gott runter
    und er singt mir was vor.
Engel weinen.
             Kunststück.

Wenn ich mal voll bin
Wenn ich mal voll bin
    geh ich kurz zum Teufel runter
    und spendier Stalin ein Bier.

Piece a cake

When I get hot, son
When I get hot, son
    I reach up and grab a cloud
    and wring it out over me.
Ice-cold shower.
                Piece a cake.

When I get cold, son
When I get cold, son
    I reach up and grab the sun
    and pop it under my coat.
Little oven.
                Piece a cake.

When I'm with her, son
When I'm with her, son
    clouds come floating down, son, with us
    and the sun comes down too.
That's love for you.
                Piece a cake.

When I get tired, son
When I get tired, son
    I reach up and grab the dear Lord
    so he'll sing me a song.
Angels weeping.
                Piece a cake.

When I get pissed, son
When I get pissed, son
    I nip down to see the devil
    and buy old Stalin a beer.

Armer Alter.

        Nebbich.

Wenn ich mal tot bin
Wenn ich mal tot bin
       werd ich Grenzer und bewache
       die Grenz zwischen Himmel und Höll.
Ausweis bitte!
        Kunststück.

Poor old bugger.
        Nebbish.

When I am dead, son
When I am dead, son
      I'll be keeping an eye on the border
      the border of heaven and hell.
Passports ready!
        Piece a cake.

Ballade vom Mann*

Es war einmal ein Mann
der trat mit seinem Fuß
mit seinem nackten Fuß
in einen Scheißhaufen.

Er ekelte sich sehr
vor seinem einen Fuß
er wollt mit diesem Fuß
kein Stück mehr weiter gehn.

Und Wasser war nicht da
zu waschen seinen Fuß
für seinen einen Fuß
war auch kein Wasser da.

Da nahm der Mann sein Beil
und hackte ab den Fuß
den Fuß hackte er ab
in Eil mit seinem Beil.

Die Eile war zu groß
er hat den saubern Fuß
er hat den falschen Fuß
in Eile abgehackt.

Da kriegte er die Wut
und faßte den Entschluß
auch noch den andern Fuß
zu hacken mit dem Beil.

* der sich eigenhändig beide Fuße abhackte

The ballad of the man*

Now once there was a man
a man who put his foot
who put his naked foot
into a lump of shit

It sickened him so much
to see his shitty foot
he vowed this shitty foot
would carry him no more.

No water could he find
to wash his shitty foot
not even for this foot
some water could he find.

So picking up his axe
and swinging at his foot
he then chopped off his foot
in haste and with his axe.

The haste it was too great
he chopped off the clean foot
he chopped off the wrong foot
in haste he chopped it off.

So he got really mad
and then made up his mind
to chop off with his axe
his other foot as well

* who chopped off both feet with his own hands

Die Füße lagen da
die Füße wurden kalt
davor saß kreideweiß
der Mann auf seinem Steiß.

Es hackte die Partei
sich ab so manchen Fuß
so manchen guten Fuß
abhackte die Partei.

Jedoch im Unterschied
zu jenem obigen Mann
wächst der Partei manchmal
der Fuß auch wieder an.

The two feet both lay there
the two feet both grew cold
the man, white as a sheet
sat by them on his seat.

The party has chopped off
a good few of its feet
a few of its good feet
the party has chopped off.

However, unlike him
the above-mentioned man
the party sometimes grows
its feet back on again.

Die hab ich satt!

1

Die kalten Frauen, die mich streicheln
Die falschen Freunde, die mir schmeicheln
Die scharf sind auf die scharfen Sachen
Und selber in die Hosen machen
In dieser durchgerissnen Stadt

    – die hab ich satt!

2

Und sagt mir mal: Wozu ist gut
Die ganze Bürokratenbrut?
Sie wälzt mit Eifer und Geschick
Dem Volke über das Genick
Der Weltgeschichte großes Rad

    – die hab ich satt!

3

Was haben wir denn an denen verlorn:
An diesen deutschen Professorn
Die wirklich manches besser wüßten
Wenn sie nicht täglich fressen müßten
Beamte! Feige! Fett und platt!

    – die hab ich satt!

4

Die Lehrer, die Rekrutenschinder
Sie brechen schon das Kreuz der Kinder
Sie pressen unter allen Fahnen
Die idealen Untertanen:

I'm sick of it

1

Cold bitches who keep kissing me
And two-faced friends who flatter me
So hot on all the hot safe bets
You shit yourselves at the slightest threat
In this city torn in two

    I'm sick of you

2

And tell me now what is the good
Of that whole bureaucratic brood
Who roll so keenly with such skill
World history's relentless wheel
Right across our people's back

    I'm sick of that

3

What would we stand to lose in those
Our famous German professors
Who really might know a thing or two
If they weren't so full of patriotic stew
Officials! Cowards! Fat and trite!

    I'm sick of it

4

The teachers, those parade-ground hacks
Who bend and break our children's backs
And with their standards fluttering
Produce the ideal underling

Gehorsam – fleißig – geistig matt
   – d i e hab ich satt!

5
Die Dichter mit der feuchten Hand
Dichten zugrund das Vaterland
Das Ungereimte reimen sie
Die Wahrheitssucher leimen sie
Dies Pack ist käuflich und aalglatt

    – d i e hab ich satt!

6
Der legendäre Kleine Mann
Der immer litt und nie gewann
Der sich gewöhnt an jeden Dreck
Kriegt er nur seinen Schweinespeck
Und träumt im Bett vom Attentat

    – d e n hab ich satt

7
Und überhaupt ist ja zum Schrein
Der ganze deutsche Skatverein
Dies dreigeteilte deutsche Land
Und was ich da an Glück auch fand
Das steht auf einem andern Blatt

    – ich hab es satt

Obedient, willing – dead in the head
    I'm sick of them

5
You poets with your clammy hands
Who rhyme to death the fatherland
Make two and two add up to five
While those after truth you bury alive
You're all for sale and slippery too

    I'm sick of you

6
You legendary little man
Who always lost and never won
Who learn to take all kinds of shit
For your daily bread you'll swallow it
Then dream in bed of bloody coups

    I'm sick of you

7
But worst of all – it makes you scream
Our German national poker game
It's not two nations here but three
And as for the happiness I see
That's written on another sheet

    I'm sick of it

Ballade auf den Dichter
François Villon

1

Mein großer Bruder Franz Villon
Wohnt bei mir mit auf Zimmer
Wenn Leute bei mir schnüffeln gehn
Versteckt Villon sich immer
Dann drückt er sich in' Kleiderschrank
Mit einer Flasche Wein
Und wartet bis die Luft rein ist
Die Luft ist nie ganz rein

Er stinkt, der Dichter, blumensüß
Muß er gerochen haben
Bevor sie ihn vor Jahr und Tag
Wie'n Hund begraben haben
Wenn mal ein guter Freund da ist
Vielleicht drei schöne Fraun
Dann steigt er aus dem Kleiderschrank
Und trinkt bis morgengraun

Und singt vielleicht auch mal ein Lied
Balladen und Geschichten
Vergißt er seinen Text, soufflier
Ich ihm aus Brechts Gedichten

2

Mein großer Bruder Franz Villon
War oftmals in den Fängen
Der Kirche und der Polizei
Die wollten ihn aufhängen

Ballad on the poet
François Villon

1

My elder brother Franz Villon
Lives in my rooms with me
When people come to sniff me out
Villon just hides away
Shut in a cupboard all hunched up
Drinking a flask of wine
He'll wait until the air is clear
He can wait a long long time

He stinks, the poet, though he must
Have smelled like some sweet bloom
Before they chucked him like a dog
Into his ancient tomb
And should a good friend come around
Three lovely girls might call
He'll jump out of the cupboard
And he'll booze until the dawn

Perhaps sometimes he'll sing a song
And ballads, two or three
If he forgets the words I prompt
Him from Brecht's poetry

2

My elder brother Franz Villon
Was often on the run
From clergy and police who both
Wanted to see him hung

Und er erzählt, er lacht und weint
Die dicke Margot dann
Bringt jedesmal zum Fluchen
Den alten alten Mann

Ich wüßte gern was die ihm tat
Doch will ich nicht drauf drängen
Ist auch schon lange her
Er hat mit seinen Bittgesängen
Mit seinen Bittgesängen hat
Villon sich oft verdrückt
Aus Schuldturm und aus Kerkerhaft
Das ist ihm gut geglückt

Mit seinen Bittgesängen zog
Er sich oft aus der Schlinge
Er wollt nicht, daß sein Hinterteil
Ihm schwer am Halse hinge

3
Die Eitelkeit der höchsten Herrn
Konnt meilenweit er riechen
Verewigt hat er manchen Arsch
In den er mußte kriechen
Doch scheißfrech war François Villon
Mein großer Zimmergast
Hat er nur freie Luft und roten
Wein geschluckt, gepraßt

Dann sang er unverschämt und schön
Wie Vögel frei im Wald
Beim Lieben und beim Klauengehn
Nun sitzt er da und lallt
Der Wodkaschnaps aus Adlershof

The old old man he'll laugh and cry
And tell some real tall tales
When he thinks of fat Margot, though
He will curse and he will wail

What did she do? I wonder, but don't
Ask too many questions
It's long ago and he
With many cunning supplications
With supplications Villon has
Quite often wriggled out
Of dungeon and imprisonment
He had luck without a doubt

With all those supplications he
Quite often 'scaped the noose
He didn't want his neck to feel
His fat arse hanging loose

3
The vanity of rulers he
Could smell from miles around
He had to crawl right up their arse
In rhyme to set it down
But still my room-mate Franz Villon
He never would shut up
As long as he had clean fresh air
Red wine and lots of grub

While procreating or while thieving
Shameless songs he'd sing
As free as any bird but now
He sits there stammering
The vodka schnaps from Adlershof

Der drückt ihm aufs Gehirn
Mühselig liest er das >ND<
(Das Deutsch tut ihn verwirrn)

Zwar hat man ihn als Kind gelehrt
Das hohe Schul-Latein
Als Mann jedoch ließ er sich mehr
Mit niederm Volke ein

4
Besucht mich abends mal Marie
Dann geht Villon solang
Spazieren auf der Mauer und
Macht dort die Posten bang
Die Kugeln gehen durch ihn durch
Doch aus den Löchern fließt
Bei Franz Villon nicht Blut heraus
Nur Rotwein sich ergießt

Dann spielt er auf dem Stacheldraht
Aus Jux die große Harfe
Die Grenzer schießen Rhythmus zu
Verschieden nach Bedarfe
Erst wenn Marie mich gegen früh
Fast ausgetrunken hat
Und steht Marie ganz leise auf
Zur Arbeit in die Stadt

Dann kommt Villon und hustet wild
Drei Pfund Patronenblei
Und flucht und spuckt und ist doch voll
Verständnis für uns zwei

Just brings on his migraine
The *Neues Deutschland*'s hard to read
(The German gives him pain)

They taught him Latin when he was
A child at school but when
Villon got older he preferred
The speech of simpler men

4
If Marie visits me at night
He kindly disappears
Goes strolling on the Wall until
The guards all shake with fear
The bullets pass right through Villon
And off the Wall they whine
But from their holes there comes no blood
Just gallons of red wine

Then for a joke he makes a harp
Out of the Wall's barbed wire
The guards ad lib accompaniment
And keep time with their fire
Then when Marie has drunk me dry
As morning comes around
And slips out silently to go
To work down in the town

It's then my good friend Franz
Comes home full of lead
And curses, spits and coughs it all up
But still smiles at the bed

5

Natürlich kam die Sache raus
Es läßt sich nichts verbergen
In unserm Land ist Ordnung groß
Wie bei den sieben Zwergen
Es schlugen gegen meine Tür
Am Morgen früh um 3
Drei Herren aus dem großen Heer
Der Volkespolizei
>Herr Biermann< – sagten sie zu mir –
>Sie sind uns wohl bekannt
Als treuer Sohn der DDR
Es ruft das Vaterland
Gestehen Sie uns ohne Scheu
Wohnt nicht seit einem Jahr
Bei Ihnen ein gewisser
Franz Fillonk mit rotem Haar?
Ein Hetzer, der uns Nacht für Nacht
In provokanter Weise
Die Grenzsoldaten bange macht<
– ich antwortete leise:

6

>Jawohl, er hat mich fast verhetzt
Mit seinen frechen Liedern
Doch sag ich Ihnen im Vertraun:
Der Schuft tut mich anwidern!
Hätt ich in diesen Tagen nicht
Kurellas Schrift gelesen
Von Kafka und der Fledermaus
Ich wär verlorn gewesen
Er sitzt im Schrank, der Hund
Ein Glück, daß Sie ihn endlich holn
Ich lief mir seine Frechheit längst

But you can't hide these things for long
And so it all came out
There's strictest Order in our land
As I quite soon found out
There came a bang upon my door
One morning just on three
Our people's grand police had sent
Three of their men to me
They said to me, "Herr Biermann,
You're well-known to us all
You're loyal to the DDR
You'll hear your country's call
Is it not true – now don't be scared –
That for about a year
There has lived here a certain Franz
Fillonk who's got red hair?
This fellow is subversive
And offers provocation
Every night to the border guards!'
– I made this declaration:

6

'Indeed it's true I almost fell
For his rude songs and tricks
But I tell you in confidence
This traitor makes me sick
And if I hadn't lately read
Korella's book which said
That Kafka was a bat
I would have met a nasty end
He's in the cupboard, glad you came
Please rid me of the pig
I gave up impudence like that

ab von den Kindersohln
Ich bin ein frommer Kirchensohn
Ein Lämmerschwänzchen bin ich
Ein stiller Bürger. Blumen nur
In Liedern sanft besing ich. <

Die Herren von der Polizei
Erbrachen dann den Schrank
Sie fanden nur Erbrochenes
Das mählich niedersank

When I was just a kid
I am a pillar of the Church
One of God's lambs am I
A solid citizen I'll sing
Of only flowers till I die.'

The cops went almost mad
Burst in the cupboard door
But all they found was a pool of sick
Seeping through the floor

Ballad of biting-mad Barbara

she kissed me and bit me un — til the blood ran · she did' not just kiss my
mouth ___ and then when I yelled she just sim-ply laughed and that's how cu
that's how and that's how I lost OUT

Leave a very long, pause in the last verse, where' · · · now
the · · · Maurie · comes, before singing on.

Soldier soldier

sol-dier soldier a hol-low form sol-dier soldier in u-ni-form sol-dier soldier
all the same sol-dier soldier it's NOT A GAME sol-dier soldier I can-not place
-dier soldier your unknown face sol-diers are i-den— ti- cal the quick, the dead

all — soldier soldier where will it lead soldier soldier **PLEASE use your HEAD** soldier soldier NO-ONE WILL WIN soldier soldier, in war again soldier soldier, the world like you soldier soldier, is young & green — but now the world has split in two and you stand in between

Guitar

soldiers are iden-

tical the quick, the dead and all

The tone is first whistled, then the rhythm is beaten out on the guitar-body so that the strings vibrate freely. Then comes the first verse, then, in A minor, the second verse, and the first verse is repeated, strummed above the bridge with a rigid middle finger.

On me and my pud in the woods

The old communist Grandma Meume's
Great Prayer in Hamburg

he ballad of Freddy Rohsmeisl, drainage-layer
om Buckow

Encouragement

don't let your-self be hardened   in these hard times of   ours

the hard ones break so easy   the sharp ones sting so ea-sy

and then are dead in   hours   and then are dead in   hours

[this is the intro and coda for the guitar]
The last verse: 'we'll make no secret of it' should be sung
slightly higher in D minor. However, if there are many
people singing the song – which is what I'd like – the last
verse can remain in A minor.

98

Moritat for Biermann's Grandma Meume in Hamburg

when my old gran was just a baby- eighty eight years a-go her mother got T B in la-bour- and to heaven she did go when my old gran was just a babe her father turned a machine on —til one day it turned on him and took his hand off c — lea — n.

The ballad of postman William L. Moore from Baltimore

SUN-DA-Y sunday meant rest for william L Moore

after a hard weeks work— he was only a postman

and pretty poor, he came from Bal-ti-more [guitar]

BLACK AND WHITE U-NITE! U-NITE! on a

placard he wrote WHITE AND BLACK HOLD RE-PRESSION

BACK!! and he set off on his own—

iece a cake

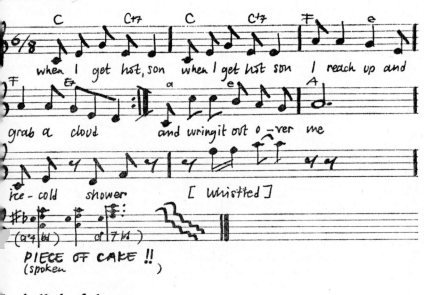

when I get hot, son   when I get hot son   I reach up and

grab a   cloud   and wring it out o — ver me

ice - cold   shower   [whistled]

(a°4 b6)   (a° 7 b6)

PIECE OF CAKE !!
(spoken   )

he ballad of the man

now   once there was a   man   a man who put his

foot   who put his naked foot   in — to a lump   of

shit   it   sickened him   so   much   to

see his shitty foot   he vowed this shitty   foot would

[GUITAR   ]

carry him no more   No   water

(etc. etc. it then goes on going up by one whole tone)

I'm sick of it

bit — ches / two-faced   who / friends who   keep / kissing / flatter   me / me   cold / and

llad on the poet François Villon

my elder   brother Franz Villon lives in my rooms with me   when people

come to sniff me out Villon just hides away shut in a' cupboard all hunched drinking a

flask of wine he'll   wait until the air is   clear he can wait a long time he stinks the etc

booze until the dawn per-haps sometimes he'll sing a song   and ballads two or

three—   if he forgets the words I prompt him   from Brecht's poetry